D0301535

ABOUT THE GOSPELS

ABOUT THE GOSPELS

BY

C. H. DODD

formerly Norris-Hulse Professor of Divinity
in the University of Cambridge

CAMBRIDGE
AT THE UNIVERSITY PRESS
1950

PUBLISHED BY
THE SYNDICS OF THE CAMBRIDGE UNIVERSITY PRESS

London Office: Bentley House, N.W.1
American Branch: New York

Agents for Canada, India, and Pakistan: Macmillan

Printed in Great Britain at the Carlyle Press, Birmingham

PREFACE

This book represents four addresses given as part of the Sunday Morning Service in the Home Programme of the B.B.C. in September and October, 1949. They are here printed virtually as they were broadcast, with the bare minimum of verbal alteration.

C. H. D.

Cambridge, November, 1949

CONTENTS

I

THE BEGINNINGS OF
GOSPEL-WRITING

The city of Rome had been devastated by a great
fire. A rumour spread among the homeless people
that it had been started by order of the Emperor
himself—the notorious Emperor Nero. An ugly
situation was developing. The government looked
about for a scapegoat. They found one in an
obscure secret society which had lately come to the
notice of the police. Its members were largely
drawn from the lower orders of the capital and
from foreign immigrants, especially Jews. They
called themselves 'Christians', after their founder,
Christus, who, the police discovered, had been put
to death on a criminal charge by Pontius Pilate,
the Governor of Judea, some years before. Clearly,
they thought, a potentially criminal organisation.
So the Christians were brought to trial on a charge
of incendiarism, with other crimes thrown in.
The Roman police had its own ways of getting

evidence, and large numbers of Christians were condemned and put to death with torture. For a time there was something like a reign of terror. Such was the first appearance of the Christian Church on the stage of world history, as it is reported by a Roman historian.

These events happened in the winter of A.D. 64-65. Shortly afterwards a little book was produced in the city of Rome under the title *The Gospel of Jesus Christ*. It contained the Christian society's own account of the events out of which it arose, and of its martyred Founder. This is the book which we know as the Gospel according to Mark. Appearing just at that moment, it had the character of a call to Christian loyalty and a challenge to a hostile world. I propose now that we should look at this short book (so far as possible) as if it were fresh from the press, and we had never read it before, and try to see what impression it makes.

The earlier chapters, I think, will appear rather scrappy. We are given a number of stories, some with an amount of picturesque detail, others brief and bald; but there is no very clear connection between them, and we are puzzled to know what is really happening. Bit by bit, however, these stories combine in our minds into a picture of Jesus of Nazareth at work in Galilee: his contacts with different types of people, and the opposition he aroused. We begin to suspect that the apparently artless story-telling has something in it of the art that conceals art, for the portrait of Jesus comes out unmistakably: his vivid and forceful speech, his poet's insight into nature and the human soul, his ready sympathy—but also on occasion his devastating severity—his integrity and strength of purpose, his power to command, and his tremendous energy. 'Gentle Jesus, meek and mild' says the old hymn, no doubt with some truth; but these are not precisely the adjectives that leap to the mind on reading Mark.

Presently the pace of the narrative gathers speed, and something like a plot begins to appear. The turning-point is at chapter viii. 27-38. Jesus, we learn, has retired beyond the frontier. Galilee has grown too hot to hold him. In his retirement he is enlisting volunteers for a dangerous enterprise. He leads them up to Jerusalem, rides into the city with a crowd at his back, clears the temple of the money-changers who do business in its courts, and challenges the ecclesiastical authorities on their own ground. They prepare to retaliate, and so we reach the final stage. With the beginning of chapter xiv the narrative takes on a fresh character. It becomes continuous, swift, and dramatic in the extreme. The loose ends of the earlier chapters are gathered up, and the reader is swept on irresistibly to the tragic climax.

It is the story of a great and good man, encircled by unscrupulous enemies, betrayed by a false friend, denied and deserted by his followers, trapped by scheming priests, condemned by a weak and vacillating judge, and put to death; but bearing himself all through with a strange dignity that wins the reluctant respect of his judge and his executioner. The story is told with extraordinary simplicity and force. There is no dwelling on grim details, and certainly no attempt to work on our feelings, yet no one with a scrap of imagination can read the story without being profoundly moved.

But when we think over it calmly, there are

many questions we should wish to ask. Who was this strange leader and martyr? What lay behind the fantastic charges brought against him? What was at issue? To answer such questions we need to have some general knowledge of the historical situation. Mark, of course, could pre-suppose such knowledge in his readers. We can only get it from history books. The scene is laid in Palestine in the late twenties or early thirties of the first century, when the country was under the Roman empire. The Jewish population bitterly resented foreign rule. The Jewish community itself was torn with political and religious dissensions. Firebrands and fanatics kept popular feeling permanently just below boiling-point, until at last it boiled over in civil war and rebellion, which brought the end of the Jewish commonwealth. The war was actually going on at the time when Mark wrote his Gospel. In the time of Jesus it was brewing up. That is the background and, the more we learn about it, the more realistic and convincing does Mark's story appear. We see Jesus, isolated from all the contending factions, both by his character and by the cause he stood for, coming into collision with first one party and then another—Pharisees, Sadducees and the rest—until they combine for a moment to destroy him before turning again to their endless quarrels. It is a straightforward and intelligible account of an episode in the history of Roman Palestine in the first century.

But it is not all plain sailing. At a first reading the dramatic sweep of the narrative may carry us along, but on a second and more deliberate reading we shall certainly be held up by some perplexing passages; and the more realistic the story becomes to us as we study it, the more forcibly the difficulties will strike our minds. Let me illustrate the kind of thing I mean.

In the course of that magnificently dramatic narrative of the closing scenes Mark records how Jesus took a last meal with his followers. He gives us homely details about the preparation for the occasion, and a report of the table-talk, laden with the emotions of parting, and shadowed by forebodings of what is afoot. It is a simple but moving scene. Suddenly Jesus breaks into the conversation with strange words. He is dividing the loaf among his guests. 'Take this', he says; 'it is my body';

and then, as he passes round a cup of wine, 'This is my blood of the covenant' (xiv. 22-24). The words come with a shock. What can they mean? We may recall that in ancient times a covenant, or solemn pact, was often consecrated by a sacrifice, which involved shedding the blood of a victim and dividing its body; and that the Jews spoke of the relation between God and his people as a 'covenant'. Then what do these words imply about the approaching death of Jesus? Do they mean that it is not merely a martyrdom, but in some way an act of sacrifice—of self-sacrifice—to bring about a new order of relations between God and man, a new covenant? Apparently they do.

Again, Jesus is being examined before the court of the High Priest. The president asks, 'Are you the Messiah?' (which we might take to mean in his mouth, 'Do you claim to be the God-appointed leader of this nation?') Jesus replies, 'I am'. But he then goes on, 'You will see the Son of Man seated at God's right hand and coming with the clouds of heaven' (xiv. 61-62). Obviously, that is the figurative picture-language which the imagination produces when we have to speak of things that lie on the far frontiers of human experience. An ancient literary tradition had used the figure of the Man on the Clouds of Heaven (shall we say 'the human form divine'?) as a symbol of the ultimate destination of human history, the final victory of the spiritual forces. Did Jesus mean something like this—'When the last fight is fought and the last victory won, you will know who I am'? Something like that, perhaps; but they are strange words from a martyr going to his death.

One more example. At the actual moment of the death of Jesus, says Mark, 'the veil of the temple was rent in two from top to bottom' (xv. 38). Again, surely the language is figurative. The 'veil of the temple' suggests that God is a 'veiled Being' hidden from us; but if the veil is rent, then something has happened which opens up the way for men to the presence of God. That 'something', Mark seems to say, happened when Jesus died.

The total effect of these passages, and many others like them, is to suggest a mysterious under-current flowing beneath the ostensible stream of events. There is more here than appears on the surface. What appears to be—and indeed is, on its own level—a story of martyrdom is also the story of something deeper; something which cannot be defined in plain words, but must be hinted at in the exalted language of the imagination; something which has to do with new relations between God and man, with the opening up of God's presence, and with the ultimate victory of the Spirit.

Mark is perfectly aware of this under-current of mystery in his story. Indeed he draws attention to it. There are ten or a dozen places where he plainly indicates that the actors in the story were in the dark; there was a secret that could not be fully divulged. In one place he calls it 'the mystery of the Kingdom of God'; and this, he says, could not be communicated to the public except in 'parables' (or figurative language) (iv. 11). It is also the secret of who Jesus really is. The question is raised again and again. Who is he? He is teacher, prophet, leader, perhaps even Messiah—but what more? That, says Mark, was his secret. It could not be fully known, even to his nearest followers, until the end of the story. So Jesus

9

moves through the scene in some sort incognito: always more than he seems. The things he does leave the spectators with a shattering conviction of the presence and power of God—unless they choose to say it is the presence and power of the devil, as some of them do. His words carry strange authority. Those who hear them either feel compelled to obey, even against their will, or else they react with unreasonable violence.

Such is the picture Mark has drawn. The actors in his drama are at a loss. There is a secret they cannot penetrate. But he has in some measure let his readers into the secret at the very outset. The first fifteen verses of his book form an introduction to the whole. They have a style and character of their own. They are packed with the picture-language of the imagination: the heavens were opened; the Spirit descended like a dove; the voice of God spoke and said: 'You are my Son, my Beloved, my Chosen!' Jesus vanished into the wilderness and fought with the devil, to return with the startling announcement: 'It is the climax of all time: God's Kingdom is upon you!' It would be wrong to attempt to reduce all this to

10

mere prose. It is the proper language for the mystery that underlies the whole story, and is the final truth of it. We are reading (Mark would have us understand) about the Son of God, invested with the Spirit of God, bringing the Kingdom of God to earth. That is what was really happening when Jesus taught in Galilee, challenged the priests in Jerusalem, and was crucified by the Romans.

But that is not the end of the story. If we have appreciated this undercurrent of mystery, we shall be prepared for the conclusion, which otherwise might appear artificial and unconvincing. Mark tells us that Jesus died and was buried; but he did not stay dead. He rose to life again, and obviously that is the true end of the story which relates how the Kingdom of God came to earth. It means that the conflict, the suffering, the apparent failure, were all incidental to a real and permanent victory of the Spirit of God, won on this earth and in history, and affecting the life and destiny of every human being. And that, I suppose, is why Mark did not call his book a *Life of Jesus*, or *Memoirs of Jesus*, but *The Gospel of Jesus Christ*;

11

for the word which we translate 'Gospel' means something like 'Good News'. But in particular it means 'News of victory.'

That is what Mark says. The question arises, 'How did he know? Can we take his word for it?' To that question we shall now turn.

II

THE LIVING TRADITION

The Gospel according to Mark, we have seen, is in all probability the earliest of the four. After reviewing the story it tells, I raised the question, How did Mark know? Can we take his word for it? Mark's book was written, I said, at Rome shortly after the great fire of A.D. 64. That is to say, it was written some thirty-five years, or a little more, after the events it records. Until then (so far as we can tell) knowledge of the facts depended on the memories of those who had witnessed them and of those whom the witnesses told. It depended on what is called 'oral tradition.'

I wonder whether you think thirty-five years a long or a short time for the memory of events to be kept alive without being recorded in writing. I fancy it is all according to one's age. When I was a young teacher of the New Testament, I remember, I used to feel this gap between event and record to be a very serious matter. Later on I realised, quite suddenly, that in my own memories thirty-five years did not seem at all a long time. It is just about thirty-five years since the outbreak of the first world war. I should like to ask any of you who are middle-aged or more: have you, or have you not, a vivid memory of what happened in July, August and September, 1914? When Mark was writing, there must have been many people about who were in their prime under Pontius Pilate, and they must have remembered the stirring and tragic events of that time at least as vividly as we remember 1914. If anyone had tried to put over an entirely imaginary or fictitious account of them, there would have been middle-aged or elderly people who would have said (as you or I might say) 'You are wasting your breath: I remember it as if it were yesterday!'.

At the same time, there is no doubt human memories are fallible, and oral tradition can go astray. We know how a good story may be 'improved' in the telling. We know how often a famous man is credited with things he never said. There is always a tendency for legends to grow up about a great man; but if the legends grow up in his own circle, among people who

14

knew the kind of person he was, these legends can throw a vivid light on his character and personality, even without being literally true. Oral tradition, in a word, can never give us anything like 'minutes of proceedings' exact to the last detail, though it can give us other things that we seldom get from minutes. But there is a margin of uncertainty. I do not think the Gospels are exempt from it. It is enough to recall that they not infrequently differ in details while agreeing in essentials. But I am now going to mention certain facts which put strict limits to the margin of uncertainty in this particular case.

To begin with, the oral tradition behind the Gospels is anything but irresponsible gossip. It is the sifted and certified tradition of a community. The early Christian Church was an intimate community and an effectively organised community. It had a strong sense both of its duty to publish its faith, and of responsibility for the truth of what it published. One of the commonest words in the New Testament is the word 'witness'. The Christian community, acting through its accredited agents—apostles, evangelists and teachers—

knew that it was on its honour to speak the truth, like a witness in court. That is the atmosphere in which the oral tradition took shape.

Further, the Christian Church grew up within the Jewish community, and only gradually separated from it. Among the Jews, the teaching of a Rabbi was preserved and transmitted by his disciples by word of mouth. They were not allowed to write it down. Obviously their memories were far better trained and more accurate than ours usually are: we are so dependent on print. The disciples of Jesus adopted the same method as a matter of course. They were not likely to be less conscientious about it than the disciples of any Jewish Rabbi. If you call to mind the teaching of Jesus as we have it in the Gospels, it is remarkable how much of it is given in forms peculiarly easy to remember. There are the parables; who could fail to remember the parable of the Lost Sheep or the Good Samaritan? There are crisp epigrams that stick in the mind like burrs: 'The Sabbath was made for man and not man for the Sabbath'; 'Whoever would be great among you shall be your servant'. 'What shall it profit a man if he gain the whole world and lose his soul?' There are whole passages that run almost like verse (in the original language they may have been in regular metre); they are nearly all complete within the compass of a few verses. In all this we can catch the accents of the living voice.

How early the tradition of the sayings of Jesus began to be written down, it is hard to say. At a guess, I should suspect it was not long after the Church moved into Greek-speaking countries. The Greeks were a bookish people, like ourselves, and liked to have things in writing. So by degrees they compiled fly-sheets with a few sayings on some special topic. Then the fly-sheets were brought together into more comprehensive collections. It seems certain that there was a considerable number of collections of sayings of Jesus in circulation. Some of them were used in the composition of the Gospels. Some we know only from quotations elsewhere. A few fly-sheets of rather later date have turned up among finds of papyri in Egypt. But all this business of writing down was only a matter of convenience. It was a by-product of the Church's system of Christian education; and this was essentially a system of teaching by word of mouth.

This fact cuts two ways, as you will see. On the one hand, the teacher had not only to repeat what Jesus said, but also to explain it to his pupils. Sometimes, it seems, the explanation was written down along with the saying itself. For example, many scholars believe (as I do myself) that the interpretation of the parable of the Sower which Mark supplies in chapter iv is not part of what Jesus said at the time, but a highly intelligent application of his parable in terms of the situation in the early Church. No doubt there are other cases. But on the other hand, the very conditions of Christian instruction offered a powerful motive for great care in distinguishing the actual sayings of Jesus from other Christian teaching built upon them.

I can best illustrate this by referring to a passage in one of Paul's letters. In the seventh chapter of the First Epistle to the Corinthians he is discussing certain questions of Christian conduct in regard to marriage and the relations of the sexes. On some points he frankly gives his opinion and commends it to their consideration. On other points he quotes what he calls a 'commandment of the Lord', and that settles the matter. 'To the married I say—not I, but the Lord: a woman must not desert her husband and a man must not divorce his wife' (vii. 11). Now the members of early Christian congregations were not all docile sheep. At Corinth in particular we know there were many who were strongly opposed to Paul and his teaching. If they could have retorted 'The Lord said nothing of the kind; you are making it up!' no doubt they would have done so. Evidently there was already a body of acknowledged sayings of Jesus, certified by those who were competent to speak; and a Christian teacher could appeal to them with confidence—and that before any Gospels were written.

So far, the tradition behind the Gospels is strictly comparable with the contemporary oral traditions of Judaism. But in one point the Christian tradition departs from the Jewish model. The disciples of Jesus not only handed down what he taught. They laid at least equal stress upon certain facts about him. When Gospels came to be written, these facts bulked largely.

Let me remind you of a passage which comes from the same letter of Paul that I referred to above (I Corinthians xv. 1-11). This letter was sent about ten or twelve years before Mark wrote his Gospel. Paul reminds the Corinthians of what he had told them when he visited them five years earlier; namely, that Christ died and was buried, and that he rose on the third day and was seen alive by Peter, James and many others; most of whom, he adds, were still alive at the time of writing. These were facts, he says, upon which all witnesses were agreed, and he had handed them on exactly as he had received them. From whom he received them, he does not say. We naturally think of the two names he mentions: Peter and James. He knew both of them. He had stayed with Peter at Jerusalem for a fortnight three or four years after the death of Jesus and during his visit he had met James too (Galatians i. 18-19). If he did not know the facts earlier (as he probably did) at any rate he learned them then. Consequently the tradition can be traced to within

20

some four years of the events and to first-hand witnesses.

In another part of the same letter (I Corinthians xi. 23-25) Paul refers again to the tradition he received and passed on. He says it included also an account of what Jesus said and did at his last supper. 'The Lord Jesus, the same night in which he was betrayed, took bread, and when he had given thanks, he broke it, and said: "Take, eat: this is my body, which is broken for you. Do this in remembrance of me".' We have already noticed Mark's account of the same occasion. We learn now that it was the custom of the Church, when it met for worship, to repeat the words and actions of Jesus, 'in remembrance of him', and to 'proclaim the Lord's death', as Paul puts it; or, in other words, to rehearse the story of the sufferings and death of Jesus, which is so movingly told by Mark. But at this time none of the Gospels was written. They drew on living memory. Sunday by Sunday, without intermission, from a time when the events were quite recent, the Christian congregation in many different places deliberately renewed the memory of facts which they could not allow to fall into oblivion. This moment of remembrance became the centre of Christian worship, and the centre about which the whole life and work of the community was shaped. So the tradition was a good deal more than the mere handing on of information. The Church not only remembered and reported the facts. It lived them. If we have understood this, we are near to the secret of the Gospels.

It is this living tradition, carefully guarded, constantly repeated, that lies behind Mark's work. That is the answer to the question: How did Mark know?

I should not care to say that everything in his book is equally close to this central tradition. He seems to have drawn on various circles and various levels of tradition. It is the task of the critical study of the Gospels to attempt to discriminate. One cannot be dogmatic about it, but many students would hold (as I do) that the strange story of the devils and the Gadarene swine in chapter v (for example) belongs to the outer fringe of the tradition and has been altered in transmission. On the other hand, such a story as that of the feeding of the five thousand in chapter vi, with all the difficulties it raises for us, and all the mystery that surrounds it, pretty certainly belongs to the ancient tradition of the centre. Whatever we may make of it, we cannot brush it aside.

And that leads me to remark that it would be a mistake to suppose that critical investigation of the tradition behind the Gospels leads us back to a simple, matter-of-fact story, without anything of the mysterious, the miraculous or the supernatural. The first Christians firmly believed that they had a story to tell which was worth telling just because it was not only about what happened under Pontius Pilate, but also about what God had done for mankind. It is in this sense that Mark tells the story, as we saw in the last chapter. We now learn that the first witnesses also told it in the same sense. Any other way of telling it would have seemed to them false to the facts as they had experienced them. If we give them another meaning, we do so on our own responsibility, and not on the evidence. There is a challenge in the Gospels, and sooner or later we are bound to face it.

III

THE DEVELOPMENT OF GOSPEL-WRITING

Although the Gospel according to Mark is pro-bably the oldest of the four, it is certainly not the best known. Both Matthew and Luke are more familiar to most of us. They are more often read in church and far more often quoted in church and out of it. It has always been so. In the second century, before the four Gospels were bound together, it seems that copies of Mark were scarce, while copies of Matthew must have been coming out as fast as the copying-staffs could deal with them, and Luke was probably not so far behind. There are obvious reasons for this; and quite good reasons. Mark has some great qualities peculiarly its own, and we value it especially because it stands nearest in time to the facts. But Matthew and Luke are much fuller. Everything that is in Mark, with the exception of a few verses, can be found also in Matthew, and two-thirds of it in Luke, while both Matthew and Luke have a good deal that is not in Mark at all. Again, in comparison with Mark, both are finished literary works, composed with care and skill. Matthew in particular is admirably constructed and arranged. Luke has style; for sheer pleasure in reading it is ahead of all the others. Both these works, in fact, represent a comparatively advanced stage in the development of Gospel-writing.

Mark had fixed the essentials of the spoken tradition in written form, happily, in the nick of time. With every year after A.D. 65 surviving eye-witnesses grew scarcer. The main currents of the Church's life continued to flow in the spoken word of worship, prayer, teaching and preaching. This living tradition still carried many memories of what Jesus said and did, over and above what Mark had written. But his book was available, its value was recognised more and more as time went on, and his example was followed. It seems that there were various further attempts at Gospel-writing, which produced nothing that has survived. But eventually the two Gospels, known to us under the names of Matthew and Luke, found universal acceptance. I should not care to give them a precise date, but if we took A.D. 75 and 95 as the limits, we should not go far wrong.

By this time the Church was becoming a numerous body. It spread to fresh fields, and aimed at wider circles. There were growing numbers of converts to be instructed, and a larger number of teachers had to be recruited. There was need for a kind of standard text-book or work of reference for teachers and pupils. Such a book should have authoritative backing, and it should give special attention to the teaching of Jesus, which was the basis on which all Christian instruction ultimately rested. The Gospel according to Matthew was designed to supply this need.

At the same time it became clear that there was a wide outside public which might better be reached through Christian literature than through street-corner preaching: the educated, reading public of the Greek-speaking cities of the Empire. The Gospel according to Luke was written primarily for this public. It is interesting to recall the preface in which he dedicated his work to a person of rank with the Greek name of Theophilus. This is how it runs:

Since many writers have attempted to compose a narrative of the events that happened among us, as the tradition of them was handed down by the original eye-witnesses and servants of the Gospel, I decided that after thorough research I would write a detailed and continuous account for your Excellency, so that you may be fully assured about matters of which you are already informed.

These two Gospels, then, stand for the two sides of the Church's work which must always be provided for, so long as the Church remains a living and active society: the instruction of its members in the Christian way of life, and the missionary appeal to the outside world. Now let us look at the two books from this point of view.

First, the Gospel according to Matthew. Its author, we will assume, wished to meet the need for an account of the life and teaching of Jesus, based on the living tradition, both spoken and written; and an account as complete as could be managed within the limits of a single roll of papyrus (the rolls were made in standard lengths). Let us see how he carried out this design.

To begin with, we can easily see that Mark's 'Gospel of Jesus Christ' is still the groundwork. In the earlier part, where Mark, as we saw, was rather rough and disjointed, the narrative has

27

been pulled about a bit and rearranged, and the language made more concise and more dignified, if sometimes less vivid. In the narrative of the closing scenes, where Mark is masterly, there is little material change, except where some extra detail is introduced. So far, we might reasonably speak of Matthew as a second edition of Mark, thoroughly revised. But into this framework of narrative the author has introduced a large number of sayings of Jesus which it was no part of Mark's design to report. Most of them (though by no means all) are grouped into five long discourses, skilfully dovetailed into the narrative at appropriate points.

The most important of these discourses is the one we call the 'Sermon on the Mount', in chapters v, vi, vii. 'Sermon' is not a very good description. It is the nearest thing we have anywhere to a systematic account of the ethical teaching of Jesus—or, as the New Testament calls it, 'The Law of Christ'. But it is not law in the sense of a code of rules and regulations which might be enforced, if necessary, by judicial penalties. The precepts of the Sermon on the Mount set before

us an ideal standard. We are never likely to reach
it fully in this life; but it remains the mark we
must aim at, and the standard by which our conduct is to be tested and judged. A very severe and
searching standard it is. If we take the 'Sermon'
by itself, we are almost driven to convince ourselves either that its precepts mean less than they
seem to say, or else that they are nice to think
about but quite unpractical. But it is rather different if we remember that the Lawgiver is also
the Hero of the Gospel story, and that the story is
about a decisive victory in the fight against evil,
which, as Mark put it, tore apart, once and for all,
the veil that hides God from us. Matthew has his
own way of saying much the same thing. In the
opening chapter of his book he says that Jesus can
best be described by giving him the name
'Emmanuel', which is Hebrew for 'God with us'.
Though the name is not mentioned again, it is
echoed in other parts of the Gospel, until in its
last verse Jesus takes leave of his followers with
the words, 'I am with you always, to the world's
end'. The Gospel, then, tells us (so Matthew
would have us understand) how God came to be

with men for good and all; and the 'Sermon on the Mount' tells us how people will wish to live who know that God is with us always, to help us keep His commandments, and to forgive us when we fail.

And now let us leave Matthew for the moment and look at the companion work. For a right estimate of the Gospel according to Luke it is well to remember that it is the first part, or volume, of a two-volume work on the beginnings of Christianity. The second volume is called 'The Acts of the Apostles'. Luke had been captivated by Paul's great idea of a genuinely universal Church, in which there should be (as Paul put it) 'neither Jew nor Greek, neither slave nor freeman, neither male nor female'. This idea inspires his enthusiastic survey of the expansion of the Church in his second volume—from Palestine, through Asia Minor and Greece, to Rome, the capital of world-empire. The same idea lies behind his first volume. He is conscious of addressing the cosmopolitan public, to which by birth and upbringing he belonged, and he puts the Gospel before them in terms which are broadly human—as it had appealed to him. From time to time he slips in unobtrusive hints that the events he is recording are not unconnected with events in the great world. Jesus was born at Bethlehem, instead of at the family home of Nazareth, because 'an order was issued by the emperor Augustus for a census of the whole civilised world'. John the Baptist began preaching 'in the fifteenth year of the reign of the emperor Tiberius, when Pontius Pilate was governor of Judaea'. When he comes to the trial of Jesus, it is the proceedings in the Roman court that interest him, and the political bearing of the charges brought—in contrast to Matthew and Mark, for whom the Jewish trial and the directly religious issues are important. Luke, in fact, is putting the story of Jesus on the map of world-history.

For his actual material, he has gone, like Matthew, to Mark, and he has made use of various collections of sayings of Jesus—one such collection, at least, which was identical with one that Matthew also used. But he had a variety of sources of information at his disposal (as he told us in the preface), and it is not surprising that we find here many incidents and sayings which are not to be found anywhere else. His choice of incidents is significant.

Here are a few of the things that Luke alone tells us. Jesus spoke up for an outcast woman in the house of a pious and censorious Pharisee. He shocked the 'ruler of the synagogue' by curing an old cripple on the sabbath day, when the congregation was assembled for worship. He caused scandal by going to dinner with the detested Head Customs Officer of Jericho. He defended his friendship with disreputable characters by telling the story of a Prodigal Son whom his father refused to disown after he had dragged the family name in the mud. He taught a Jewish lawyer what it means to be a good neighbour by a story about a generous Samaritan—the point being that Jews and Samaritans lived cheek by jowl in the same little country, and hated one another as only close neighbours can. Luke has several of these stories about Samaritans. He liked them because they showed how Jesus broke down barriers, and there he saw the possibility and promise of a universal society of mankind, such as the Church was des-

tined to become. All through the book, we are
struck by the note of warm human feeling, in
contrast to a certain austerity in Matthew. It is
hardly accidental that so many of Luke's scenes
are laid at a dinner-table, while Matthew prefers
scenes where Jesus is on a mountain-top. We
might put it this way: if in Mark Jesus appears as
the heroic Leader, and in Matthew as the great
Teacher and Law-giver, in Luke he is above all
the Friend of Humanity.

The Gospel according to Luke, then, is a 'missionary' book. But I must not leave the impression
that Matthew is not. So let us finish by looking at
Matthew once again. It is true that he is pre-
occupied with the instruction of the Church's own
members in the Christian way of life. But he is
certainly not thinking of the Church as a closed
society, absorbed in its own efforts after perfection.
He makes it quite clear that the Church is being
trained for responsibility towards the world in
general. 'You are the salt of the earth . . . you are
the light of the world', says Jesus in the 'Sermon
on the Mount'. But it is at the very end of the
Gospel that this world-outlook comes out in a

startling way. Jesus appears, alive after death, invested with supreme command over the human race, and commissions his disciples, like the envoys of a king, to call his subjects to their allegiance. These are his words: 'I have been given all authority in heaven and earth. Go: make all nations my disciples, and teach them to keep all the commands I have given you'. It is a quite shattering commission, to these eleven plain men of Galilee; but it is the logical conclusion of the whole Gospel, according to Matthew and Luke alike.

THE INTERPRETATION OF
THE GOSPEL

If you are familiar with the first three Gospels, you feel a certain strangeness when you come to the Gospel according to John. It is not only that it describes different incidents, or the same incidents in different connections; and it is not only that the teaching of Jesus is reported in a different style and manner, or that it deals in part with different topics; though these differences are clear enough. But it is the general contrast of tone and 'atmosphere' that is so striking. The chief reason for this is that John has aimed at giving an interpretation of the life of Jesus rather than one more record, and an interpretation for a new public.

His book was published not far from A.D. 100. By the end of the first century the Church's movement of expansion was proving astonishingly successful. There were well-rooted Christian communities in most of the big cities of the eastern Mediterranean, some of them as much as half a century old. They made themselves felt in their localities. Each community developed its own life and organisation with the vigour of a local growth, and each became a centre from which fresh advances were made. In many of these cities there were groups of serious and open-minded people, awake to the deeper problems of life, often under the influence of Greek philosophy, who were moving away from the popular paganism and seeking a purer and more spiritual way of religion. Christian teachers early made contact with such circles, and took pains to present the faith in ways which could appeal to them. John has clearly had such people in view in writing his Gospel.

It was written, so ancient writers credibly nform us, at the Greek city of Ephesus in Asia Minor. So it was intended for a public for whom the events of the life of Jesus were almost ancient history, and a public far removed geographically from the scenes in which they had taken place; even farther removed perhaps in intellectual climate. In writing for them the evangelist has also written for us (we may say). We are even farther away, in time and place, from first-century

Palestine. If we read the fourth Gospel as it was meant to be read by its first readers, we may learn from it that Jesus Christ is not merely a figure in ancient history, but the eternal Contemporary.

Here is one example of the way John re-tells the story, for his new public. Mark and the others recorded that Jesus was condemned by a Roman provincial court on the charge of claiming to be 'king of the Jews'—a charge amounting to high treason. One can imagine a reader saying to himself, 'What does it matter to me who was king of the Jews sixty years ago—or nineteen hundred years ago?' But see how John reports Pilate's examination of his Prisoner (xviii. 33-37). I will paraphrase it slightly to bring out the points.

Pilate: Are you the King of the Jews?

The Prisoner: Are you using the word 'king' as you would use it yourself, or did someone else put the word into your mouth?

Pilate: Do you take me for a Jew? It is your own people who say you claim to be a king.

The Prisoner : If I were a king as you are using the word, I should not have been taken prisoner without a fight. But my kingdom is not that kind.

37

Pilate : Then you admit you claim to be a king?

The Prisoner: 'King' is your word, not mine. My mission in the world is to bear witness to the truth. My subjects are those who are loyal to the truth.

Pilate (scornfully): Truth! What is truth?

Your Greek reader of the second century—or your English reader of the twentieth—should understand that well enough, and find it relevant.

Here is another example, of a rather different kind. You will recall the scene in Mark where Jesus fed a multitude of people with bread in the wilderness. Mark observes, with some emphasis, that there was something about it which no one understood at the time. John re-tells the story in his own way (vi. 1-14); but instead of leaving it with a cryptic hint of a secret not divulged, he appends a long discourse on the theme of 'bread of life'; by which he means the invisible, divine powers that nourish the spiritual life of men. The secret, he says, is that Christ opened up fresh sources of spiritual nourishment; or rather, that Christ is himself the source of spiritual nourishment. The reader is thus encouraged not to think so much about what happened by the Sea of Galilee one evening in March about A.D. 30, but to consider what it is to be spiritually starved, and to learn how Christ satisfies the hunger of the soul. In a word, the incident has become what John calls a 'sign', or symbol, of something which is true always and everywhere, and which the reader, whoever he is, can prove in his own experience.

In this way, all the actions of Jesus that John records—and he gives only a small selection compared with the wealth of incident in the other Gospels—are treated as 'signs', or symbols, of some deeper truth. When Christ cleanses the temple, it is a sign that the old way of religion, with its sacrifices and ceremonies, gives place to the worship of God 'in spirit and in truth'. When he gives sight to a blind man, it means that he enlightens the spiritually blind with the light of truth. When he raises dead Lazarus to life, it stands for the awakening of the spiritually dead to a life worthy of the name.

To say that these events are symbolic does not, of course, mean that they are imaginary, or that they never happened as events in history. You will remember that I called attention to the 'mysterious under-current' that runs beneath Mark's simple story; and not only Mark's story; in all forms of the living tradition, as far back as we can trace it, the story always moves on these two levels. It is about what happened 'under Pontius Pilate', and it is about what God has done for mankind. Now John, as I understand him, argued somewhat in this way: If the total effect of this whole episode in history was to disclose God working behind the scenes, then it should be possible to detect traces of the divine action in every single thing that Jesus said and did. Accordingly, he has soaked himself in the tradition, and meditated over and over again on every incident it related. Possibly he read the other Gospels, though I see no compelling reason why he should have done so. Gradually, as he meditated, over a period of years, one incident and another became transparent, and he saw the underlying pattern behind the mere occurrences as tradition reported them. And so, in composing his Gospel, he has re-told these incidents in such a way as to bring out the inner meaning of each of them separately and of the story as a whole. He has done this by a combination of three methods; partly by re-shaping the stories themselves in detail, partly by arranging them in a special order, which is not necessarily the order of time in which they happened, and partly by placing alongside a story a discourse which expounds its deeper meaning. Mark was always hinting at a secret—'the mystery of the Kingdom of God'. John has told the secret, perhaps as fully as it can be told.

What he gives us is no ordinary narrative, where one thing follows another in a simple succession. The links that connect one episode with another are extremely subtle. It is rather like a musical fugue. A theme is announced, and developed up to a point; then a second theme is introduced, and interwoven with the first, then perhaps a third, with fresh interweaving, until an intricate pattern is evolved, which yet has the unity of a consummate work of art. The Fourth Gospel is more than any of the others an artistic and imaginative whole.

The thought that runs through it all is gathered up in brief in the preface or prologue (i. 1-14).

41

The prologue is about God's self-revelation. Only John does not use any such cumbrous term. He speaks simply of 'the Word'; appropriately enough, surely; for a word is the normal means by which a person communicates with another person, to make known what is in his mind. The question is, how does the eternal God communicate with us, and let us know what is in His mind? John's answer is that what is in the mind of God—His thought, His purpose—is expressed in the whole of His creation, more especially in the life of living things, and most of all in the thinking mind of man. And not only has He thus revealed Himself in the standing constitution of nature and of man; His Word has also 'come' to men in history in special ways, through the work of prophets and men of God. Consequently, it is possible to hear God speaking to us over the whole range of nature, history, and human experience. But unfortunately it is also possible to know a great deal about nature, its order and beauty; to know a great deal about the wonderful working of the human mind; and even to be well acquainted with the teaching of prophets and sages—and yet never to 'receive the

Word', as John puts it; never to hear God speaking *to us*. 'He was in the world', says John, 'and the world was made by Him—but the world did not know Him'. And the indictment is surely just. Then, finally, God spoke in a human life: 'the Word was made flesh'. So the meaning which all creation holds, if we could only see it, is precisely the meaning of this story of Jesus: what he did, what he said, how he suffered, died and rose to life. If we knew what all that means, we should know what God means by this universe, and what He means by our own lives in His universe.

Now we understand why John insists that we shall pause over every single incident as we go through the story, until we have got below the surface and seen what it means. Each incident is a place where we may hear the eternal Word spoken, which interprets to us our own lives and the whole universe of our experience. In one sense, each several incident contains the whole truth of the Gospel, as John unfolds it; and yet, as we read, we are aware of movement and progression. We are being led step by step towards a climax. The climax comes in the latter part of the book, where the author tells once again the story of the sufferings, death and resurrection of Jesus Christ, and sets forth after his own manner the meaning of these momentous events.

The narrative itself, in chapter xviii and the following chapters, is plain, realistic, full of dramatic detail. It does not exactly reproduce the account given in the other Gospels. It has every appearance of being a fresh and original rendering of the Church's memory of the facts, as it was preserved in the living tradition. Here and there the attentive reader will notice unobtrusive pointers to a deeper meaning, but they are never allowed to interrupt the flow of the narrative. But John expects us to read the story with understanding; and he has the right to expect it, because he has already given us, in the five chapters which immediately precede, what amounts to a penetrating commentary on the events. His method of accompanying the record of an incident with a discourse explaining its meaning is here employed on the grand scale.

In chapter xiii John, like the other evangelists, is recording the last supper of Jesus with his followers, and the table-talk on that sorrowful occasion. Gradually the familiar table-talk takes a different tone, as Jesus begins to speak to his disciples of what lies before him, and of what it means for them and the world. Slowly, meditatively, the discourse moves from point to point, exploring one aspect after another of its great theme—the benefits of Christ's passion. Conversation gives place to prophetic utterance. Finally (in chapter xvii) it rises into prayer; for it is only in the language of prayer that the last truths of religion find fitting expression. I will quote a few phrases from the prayer:

> For their sake I consecrate myself, that they too may be consecrated in the truth . . . that they may all be one, as thou, Father, art in me, and I in thee, that they may be in us . . . made perfectly one.

I will not attempt to comment on that. It is the conclusion of the whole matter.